SCORCHING CRUCIBLE

"THE WISE WISDOM"

KUMAR ABHISHEK

Copyright © Kumar Abhishek
All Rights Reserved.

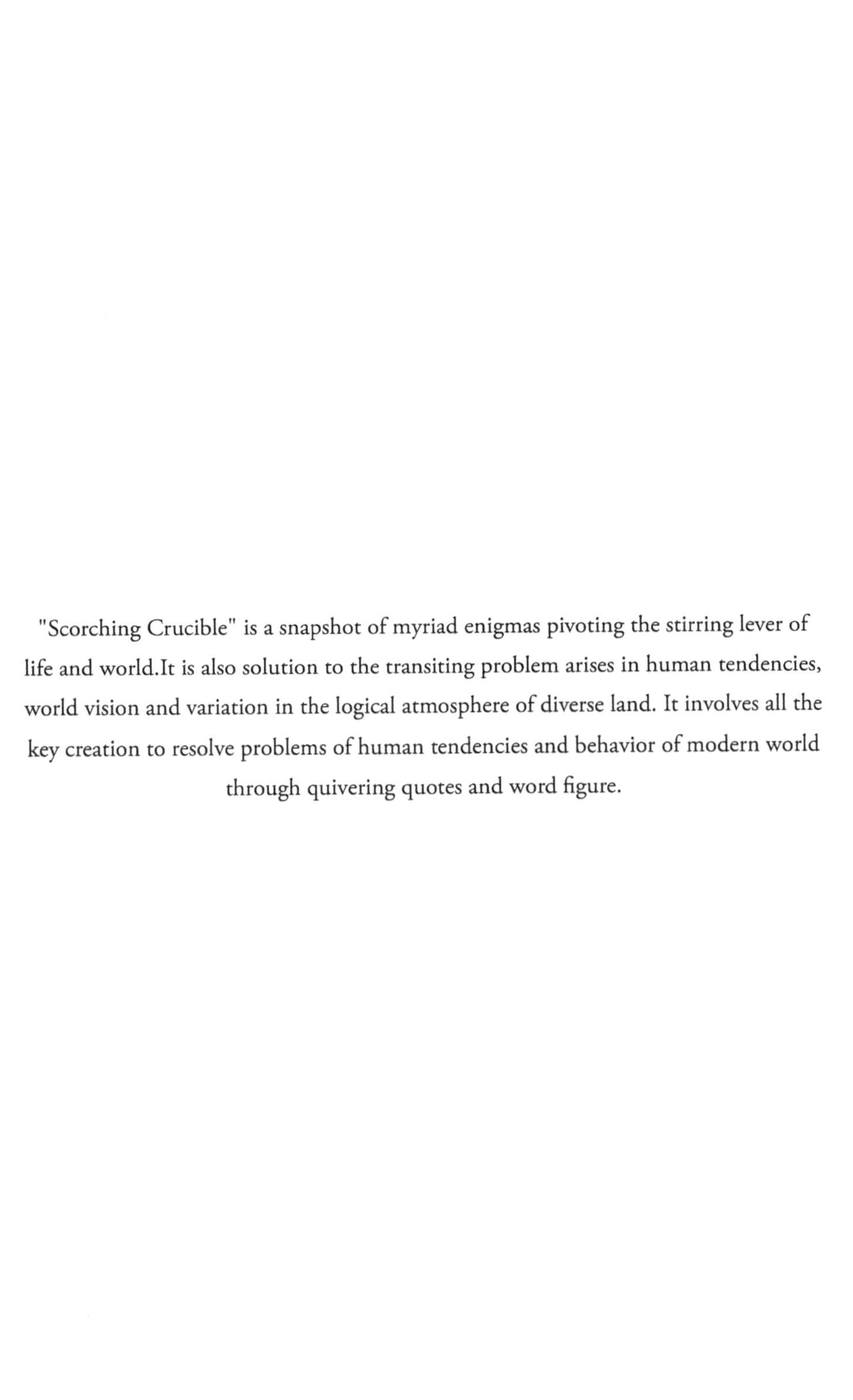

"Scorching Crucible" is a snapshot of myriad enigmas pivoting the stirring lever of life and world.It is also solution to the transiting problem arises in human tendencies, world vision and variation in the logical atmosphere of diverse land. It involves all the key creation to resolve problems of human tendencies and behavior of modern world through quivering quotes and word figure.

Contents

Contents

Preface

Language Of Awakening

Poetry is a language of awakening,

Awakening the sense of regular darkening,

It involves you in it very quickly,

Like color in water very thinly and weekly,

Poetry has a sense of belief in it,

A belief that characterize like leaf of a tree retreat,

A belief that is hard, smell like a slow work,

That is revolving like a star around a galaxy like a political talk,

A belief about investigating a case by a surgeon,

Which in case is a brain's devil region,

Life gives opportunity to everyone to threshold,

Not once, twice but many times in hoard,

Which is hidden inside our own travelling &destiny glance,

Yes we need to glance our destiny by enlarging mirror,

Like in a marathon first we run slow than glance fast to be a winner.

1. FLYING IN THE MASQUERADE LIFE

Flying in a masquerade life of dream,
In the midst of mean delight with whim,
Passed many universe of logistic life,
Whirled rings of unknown light pipe,
Carrying moments of infinite millers,
Shrinked in frequent indefinite colors,
Light haven life crawled in my eye,
Chirped calmly, loosing all tense tie;
What and when charmed your spirit,
And come so far in a idle spright,
Oh! there truesome melody of ease,
Nectar and divine like heavenly bees:-
No ego, no pride, no tracking, no stride,
Rare and intense still evenly bright,
Coordinated and united from mere mass,
Like sprinkled musk on a flower vase,
Lights liquored my eyes in a poesy ride,
Lights loaded my sight like passion guide,
Lights luminescent my thoughts as true,
Lights as energy token with vision too-
And, revealed there identity of 'mere mass'
Energy particles with invisible speed jazz,
Unrelated till observed by some visible odd;
Weighed atomics when transform to work,
Frequently spinning from mere mass on torque,
And the fountain of infinite energy enter;

In the core chambers of my heart,
Filled it with love, life, energy and light,
And excited it to exile more trivially,
Drawn my passion, my sorrow aright,
Then things seemed stalled and bright,
That Trance things of my counting heart,
Mattered my mind in that spacial craft,
That holds a few petals of beauty beam,
Obluted it to mean the located dream,
That rationalise my spirit to swing ,
And randomised all things with the wing,
Dotted discretely in my digital heart,
To commune to the source of infinite light,
Where all matter hold and release,
Where all time and all space cease,
With ease and the end at the same point,
To attain, getting the throughput joint;
Of cosmic energies that holds it to sink,
Of varied lengthy waves in different link,
Between the discrete digital heart,
While mapping the meaning of grace impart,
And i remained in light in pomp receive,
Transiting self to joy and retrieve,
Approached to tether in the perennial searching,
Stopped somewhere in a bay of heart beating,
And this part of dream burst to keen light,
As dreams were refracted to a drowsy flight,
To find a lolling world of passion hearted,
Rode upon several small spheres' departed,
The new bay was on the 'source' sphere;
Like influential spin ball of infinite energy,

Ideally auspicious, the solace source was breezy,
In and out of eternity like some system priority,
Rotating as a point star of bright gravity,
Holding me and the whole system with innate glee-
A influential spin ball with infinite energy,
And the winged lights belong to the source,
The bright bay was their hoarded house,
Therefore, stalled in my trivial eyes,
To illuminate the path of diabolic dice,
Witnessed a nystanthes dream disc to trivial star,
As it was having great hot fountain afar,
Of instant enlightenment, most palpable,
And thundering loud that a human hardly,
Resist, disable to ponder and reach inly,
But the inside enlightenment's provided,
With inertia, moment, and desires' glided,
Which when entered into me and pause,
For a cause to reach their bay house,
And the cause was its effect and creation,
Its zonal system and their differentiation,
With all its gravity tool of influence,
That hold them together in accordance,
All things are at its entreme,
Outflowed me to swift at extreme
Broadened my vision to search all nook,
Every prospect of all grayish look!
O! that whizz in all the solitary planets,
Outspread all the light leafs to measure,
The differentiation of all peering world,
And there were several world of lights,
And one enwritten natural world like earth,

Where people, prank and puzzles get birth,
Living organisms live in light favour,
After death, grounded or absorbed in air,
In due course of fairy wings of fairer world,
Viewed the tenantless desert where lights hurled,
By the shining source in the sleeping glade mode-
A gazer of sleepy system in the dream disc pod,
Refracted: the hot breath and the cold death-
Seen a white crude mass of mercurious flow;
Rays reflecting and transmitting the soul,
From the white source soul to planet pearl,
Reflecting rays of oval angular curl,
Anchored realms on the lightening meteor,
Illuminated spheres enhanced from the core,
A crystal planet of voluminous air, very vigorous;
Withhold dense clouds, static and glamorous,
In volcanoes of charm and beauty annexure,
With reflective hot air, showing love of its nature,
On an unexplained plain of beauty curve,
With glaze and glow of many arteries and nerve,
Reminded me of the trial beating heart,
In every texture and bidding part,
And the breaking emotions on reflective rocks,
Unbounded in nature like a devil mocks,
Extending my vision to a another core,
With lifeless dust and life no more,
Reached a small rocky red planet,
Of real red radiant, absorbing the heat horizon,
At the near separation as a terror season,
Like sunset in the old crude silent ocean,
Perceptual to extremes of ancient ion,

With never ending bloodshed of radical war,
Restricting life, medieval but soully very far,
And not let living to make love like star do,
Impassive, ever-extinct by source as morning dew,
Standing on the beautiful bay in course,
And travelling accessibly via light source,
Crawled and searched another giant mass;
Of giant gravial rocks, a planet jumbo,
With many faint white rocks like crescendo,
With only and many moonly brightness afar,
And faint freezing rocks far from the source star,
Rolled and rilled, round after round,
Stooped and shrinked above dense ground,
By the ventilated and veined wing,
Which was dense, whiled like a eternal ring,
Freezing and floating in its lofty space,
With wisdom of genuine gusty wind trace,
That they takes to the dreaded nest,
Let them to oppose the stationary rest,
A dark giant planet deprived of bright door,
With self electrifying world of aromatic core,
Freeze faint rocks, hanged in its outer world,
Like lustrous flowed solid metal get mold,
And the shattered rings, flew and bound,
Igniting scarlet firewall, swiftly moved around,
To re-energize the storms of the cluttered cloud,
Which they possessed to loose, whatever clawed,
When along with lights crawled like a beetle,
On a gas giant mass of low clouds in every nodal,
Of the unanimous sky of numerous moon,
The ring systems tilted sideways and immune,

Because of a magnetosphere in its timed core,
Thus, formed an archery board of freezing ore,
Hanged to be hit by any roaming ray,
Or a fleeting object shadow from the bay,
Travelling with the speed of light:
Far form the temporal source star,
When the ventilation of speedy wind shutter,
Non-existed in uncontrolled icy touch of nature,
Without any lime lite and rocky creatures,
And every curve of hills and mountain feast,
Reminded me of the romantic beauty crest,
A vast sea of ripples and plain tunes like hurdle,
And the fumed, freeze cold, hold the air girdle,
That fascinate my thoughts to heroic glaze,
As the planet itself symbolically says-
"A vast sea film of rebels and romantic rocks",
All faint and fragmented without light knocks,
And the fragrance of soul on those bluish rocks;
Of night jasmines' curves hurdled me to stall,
Of each night jasmines', curved in a whole,
Hurdling to stair back to source soul,
With the fragrance of soul on sigh bluish rocks,
Of night jasmines' swimming atmosphere, shores,
Inserted the nozzle of lights served over sphere,
And allowed to squench the natural beauty curves,
At the mean time of the time travel:
In the mean position of the travelled tail,
From the static and dynamic drawing source,
Architected lifeless rocks in circular course,
Realized and propelled with the speed of light,
In the constant ride of indispensable insight,

And fell on the blue lustrous logging world,
Free from rationalised system like sold,
Carrying life and light of spectroscopic molten matter,
Heaved by the flowing orientation of liquid crystal,
Reflected its blue soul in exponential sky,
Gradually, formed its atmosphere and imply-
Densely differentiated formed that crude core,
Densely differentiated from the crude source;
Of lustre of ductile rays and value peeved,
To animate all shadows from the source,
And enter into its atmospheric pores,
Then the differentiated planet got the living,
Through out the existed enamours of loving being,
And produced and mapped into reality,
In the madrigal of life, stoically and duality,
With all ecstasy of the decimal descent sky,
Briefed and differentiated by the source's spy,
Its high sounding effect on all land,
The eternity of soul in every trend,
And let the species to indulge in life trade;
In love, birth, talk walk, on death fade,
That, what was the scheme of the system?
How life had been prepared by the source?
How soul had been inferred in sigh rocks and ores?
And existed the live characters in animation,
Within infinite soul, the 'fleshy one' creation,
The fleshy one rationalized and sublimed in mysteries,
Mapped into many and multiple histories,
Stirred the planet pot with green gripper,
Created the land, boundary and the ethereal air,
To inspire the flashy one and their kind,

Weaving world of lives, enshrined and rewind,
Therefore, the then cycle started by the source,
To exert love and life in living course,
Hence differentiated the whole entropy of planet,
In the scrapbook of integrated matrix plant,
From the bay of self solace source:
Lights sailed on living being,
Their godly effects on them on wing,
Of auspicious spirituality, emerging prime,
With due respect to space and time,
The primary ray begun in the nodal hold,
Brightened a part of its easterly world,
Shadowing each and all within soul,
And clicked each and all the whole,
Reflected the shadowed image of the mused,
In the first land, rays ardently arrive,
Of the first flag in the nook on a small hive,
Mutating them with caressing colours of sight,
In light hearted way and alluring white,
And those fleshy one, immortal and implored,
By the tireless solace source, timed and encored,
Explored the eternal, ethereal, early morn,
Whiffed the breeze to swirl the flower corn,
Like ardent orchard placed before mist of light,
Getting evolved by the spirit of morning byte,
Myriad, light weighted, full of fragrance and tone,
Unresistant to tiny water droplets in hanging environ,
And its squeezing aroma on every chilled lawn,
Feeling of passionate love of dew at the dawn,
Embracing the environs to its fullest,
And when the bright effervescent lights came,

The sizzling sigh dew vanished from the game,
To let them to grow in mercuric light flow,
And charmed with its cosmic colours of glow,
On diversified and differentiated planet;
Lights, with its inevitable and enhanced effect,
Wishing within white, inside and out enact,
All, looking for a media to transform into and over,
Extremes of sky sea's Crystal and red radical flower,
And the green to hold the environs,
Yellow showing the eternity in turbulent tyrants,
So, ever radiant, flexible and mighty lights,
Reflected colours to the planet's sights,
After all, missing the truism of true white light,
Devoid of renunciation, to a different height,
Left it in falsehood to serve 'fleshy one',
To live in parted way, and not to be shun,
And deceivingly apart ed from the truth,
Like a butterfly, actually a meandering moth,
Acquired the quantum of light and environs,
Moving tactically in dream's vacuum, without siren,
To whom? Overcast fringes of lives-
To the awakened sublimed central infringe,
The inner self soul, beyond brightness and free,
From the outer flesh; a dark boundary,
Darkened by falsehood with only true whole soul,
In self, and the Single Soul of all, in all,
Union of everything, enduring, one and the only,
Holding each and infinite number of keys,
Of millions of million, source and sink trees,
Residing beyond all called almighty,
Who entangled, tuned heart inside fleshy one,

With strange, tuned fringes of light cone,
And hidden beyond all odd, even omnipresent,
In the rarest clue of each tremendous effect,
The primitive source brightened every clue;
To the lustrous affinity of the planet blue,
Of the deep wide flowing liquid to the big pores,
Of the reflected image of infinite blue universe,
Covered the major surface on its canvass guide,
And those cornered universal rocks beside,
The vast oceans, tempered to touch the rock;
Settled in entropy of time, gathered to knock,
Where the abyss gaps vanish in tabulated time,
The aroused waves came to crash in rhyme,
With the mighty rocks or damped like wine,
Paddled in the soaking soil of bold beaches crust,
Mean while the rocks hardly tranquilize its thirst,
When the egocentric, jealous, broad beach,
Let them to meet when intervened by sky's witch,
Traveling spiritually like the waves of the seas,
To find the ever diminished destination devotees,
And i saw my true image, reflected,
Travelling in the indefinite dreams' parted,
A journey on the stirred lights on spiritual waves:
To find a destination of dream within a dream,
In a tribal ship with hope as the only prism,
And alone captain of the ship travelled tirelessly,
Depicting the vast spiritual, truesome oceans' fairy,
A ship was about to move,
Withholding memory dust,
Passing shores, fluently flowed,
To scorch captain's mind rust,

When the turbine twirl the spirit,
With high sounding satiated waves,
Switched and headed along by stream,
By stalking, what moment, it heads,
The sky was orange in a chilled evening,
In the rationalised sky and roaming breeze,
Mixed into the battled blue orient ocean,
Merging all the love song at dusk whizz,
Exponential To many life's lingering labour,
Where birds and rain play in sobre sky,
Their eternal game of hide and seek,
Singing the song of destiny on a sly,
The captain in the coral water, sailing duly,
With only compassionate corona as a compass,
With hefty hope of digraph destination,
Tackling each obstacle in the bio-scope canvass,
How come the captain sailed to pored ocean,
Of its large, thick blue lustrous tribal tide,
Deep and ceased in its winsome freedom,
And the passive fluent water, imperial and pride,
Involving and evolving the fortuitous organisms,
Finned to overcome dense, pivoted water,
Poured and packed in pores of blues,
To invent a viscous slippery system of charter,
Passed many sovereign sea of lustrous character,
In deeply dodged, careens of volcanic stream,
Where large turrets of ocean, grown glimmers,
Freely encashed to extremes, in life cycle's prism,
An indigenous sky's colored sea of open eddies,
Endoscopic, interviewed, invariance improved to imply,
With an equanimity of gradiance to the organism,

Hale and hearty in their chain beneath the stooped sky,
In the shore of a amid analytical sea,
Of mighty white organisms in lustrous love,
And the stalwarts were vanquishing their soul,
From every seashore, followed to cove,
Following the northern norton star,
Somehow, the cabled captain came to the cold age,
An ocean of mighty polarised organisms without fear,
Articulated in antiquity of time's cage,
Passing tirelessly, came to the opposite pole,
Full of freezed and freed Aquarius fragment,
Adaptation of aquatic blues in white snowfall,
There was nothing, and nothingness of tolerance intent,
Travelling patiently in the ocean's wisdom,
Creating short ripples on the ocean of time,
Collecting the hoary antiquity of its glory,
Of the congruent characters in the varied regime,
On impulsive thoughts of cordial waves,
Seeking and cycling a strange philosophy,
The oneness of things in the organic ocean,
A real proof of the organic rationality,
The captains hunt for treasure diminished
When the treasures found in life seemed,
Only a dust of intolerance and desire,
The inside darkness, absorbed and screamed,
And the hidden streams throughout,
The glorious journey on time's measure-
How wonder full rational streams were,
An insight support like the true treasure!-
That how the oceans, come down,
Permeated in the planet's prism,

Outcasted and boasted the civilization,
A treasure of rationalised wisdom!
All things, transparent from the divine source,
The oceans, seashores, lustrous love endorse,
A coloured wet tune of a cosmic string,
The viscous volume permeated in the planet,
And the universe itself like a drop bloom,
Of the transcend ocean of glory and gloom,
Of the soul beyond time and space trace,
Installed into the coloured fleshy one to grace,
In the contentment of fragmented water and land,
Differentiated in different forms from source's bay,
By the mystic rays swinging inside and away,
Seen the evolution from the steadfast star,
Of the first effect on planet, light and bright,
With rummaging choices in passion plight,
Fleshy one, divided their water and lands,
And hopeful civilizations take birth in trends,
In the joint land mass of generation miracles,
Responding and retorting in the life cycles,
One was the light visionary social culture;
Growing in the ceramic land of modern duty,
Well suited to the philosophy of necessity,
Similar to workaholic ants, bound to work,
Within a high spirit, like speedily shuttling cork,
When the focus reaches on the another glimpse;
Radiating energy in lives shells of modern dreams,
Of different reasoning and passionate tirades,
Residing in large flora over its vast lands,
In beautiful roving rainbows of life's legacy,
When the lights intensed on a rational ecstasy;

A land of quick morning in the burst light,
Like an ancient sparrow of rusted wing,
Trying to sport its color of spiritual swing,
Stretching the wings for its flight on autumn eve,
In the diverse land like vivid sunflowers, instinctive,
Calculated in aroma of universal cultural flood,
From infinite inverse time, lingered thoughts world,
Performing spirituality of light from eternity,
Of soul, pulsating and eccentrically encored,
Few eccentric ray particulate to beauteous apart-
To the separate content land in its bound,
Beseech and appraised by ocean around,
Where blue sky bends in joy crest,
Mighty fleshy one in mid and dim forest,
Were fair and bright in vision sweet,
As the lights get intenser with rotating planet;
The chored and intensed fleshy one established,
In ionic lands of dashed and dotted soils,
And azzureous world of their keen kind,
Materialistic spirituality to crusty bind,
When stupendous light of source at the mast
In the progressing planet of heat heaved in cast,
Effected from the radiant radical soil,
Yet their tumultuous triumph to toil,
For change of cultural disbelief in olden strife's,
With total abandonment and passionate kites,
In the edging corners of its vertical world,
To fly passionately in the stumbled studs,
And absorbed in the operatic augmented rock,
When the bright lights pulsated to poke;
The euphoric realization of logical world,

Where practice and practical of fleshy one,
Triumphed and stretched in fullest fun,
Imbibing differences of opinion invasion,
In the modern advancement and its realization,
Fascinated the green living culture in the planet,
In the broad spectrum and shrinked scarlet,
Fleshy one flourishes in deep conviction,
To earnestness of the reality and fiction,
In the indefinite flow of the rays horizon;
An eternal dark land of nature's horn,
Where indigo lights of the mortal moon,
Follow darkness to affirm tides as soon,
As the sober rays ventilated in eyes,
Over the dark corona, supporting lights,
Murmuring in the nature's lap and rivers,
Caressing misty rains over the green grime,
Truest and fathoming from ageless time,
Possessing the eternity of heaven; of joy,
Of dreamer and wanderer; not to destroy,
A lovelier and happier kind of color bound,
And tribal tags with their identity around,
When the stirred lights arrived swiftly;
On astonishing aimed land of typical monotony:
In unified and colorful glory, on the planets wall,
To bind in one glowing bosom hall,
Beetling in the wondrous shiny ray,
On the chaos iron world of red time array,
A bright impression falling from Solemn sky,
Encumbered in dew of chilling chronicle eve-
And the moonly beam adored them to give:
Some were silken damsel bright,

Some were shadowy moonlight kite,
Glittered and entangled in the rich land,
One after one, seen all kinds of fleshy one,
All in untied gratitude, vision amain!
In great unity, and relaxed in countenance,
With all dreadful and murderous weapons,
Established in the constraint of lights cranes-
Among the dreaded, wilderness of peace!
And the differentiated power-pron planet,
Interns as the strife-torn planet, non-offended-
Ah! with sorrow and grace, defined and blended,
Trapped me to hear, the shadow of lonesome melody,
Bad! lowly tone in the vacuum dream's custody;
All in contempt of disgrace!
And my swelled thoughts found nothing to praise,
Decided: that was the hidden hope, pale and mild,
Abrupt tones of nature; fleshy one, the source's child,
Also with some intoxication, and few joy and pride,
Glittering and twinkling on the planet's ride,
Standing alone at the bay of light's source,
of different sights; its vision force,
Flying in the masquerade life-
Travelling tirelessly in the temporariness of temporary world,
In colorlessness of dreams,
Authenticated and agitated me to asleep,
And then I relised this is the crude color of life which creeps,
And scroll in the surface of sometimes upwards of the planet,
And sometimes triggers the slope deep.

2. ANATOMY OF ATALL SOUL EXTOL

It starts with a night of a Stall Soul,

Seemingly seamed only echo reside beside,

In that dark night like deep torque,

Sky vanished, shorted a dark premise,

Moon denied to spread its delight,

Nothing in the night,

Not even a wandering star,

A long, a lot dark afar,

To saw few dwelling in that furious night,

And Stall Soul was shelling in search of light,

Incense dark, it was;

Trying time of temporary dark,

Inferring through eternity,

The dark and Stall Soul, amid singularity,

And the only prevailed parity,

When Stall Soul was roaming in that immemorial night;

Of realms of volcanic emotions fight,

Of duly restless energy of psyche Stall Soul,

Mapping and resembling the inertial call,

Provided reluctance and reflectance with respect to time,

Buried time, hard to disclose, unless it is prime,

Which was affirming the startling of a star

Brightened the visuals, flashing all regime,

Fixing and wondering it for every dwelling spirit,

Prepared a temptation, that gain a blast evolving heat,

Stall Soul approached, up-roared, and remain self poured,

Every unique drop of ether shake of molten ray,
Concealing a circular capillary, that he kept away,
Darkness raised, Stall Soul had a promise to dealt,
Every night he had drunk the shacked ether,
That was the final call of eternity,
To bond with hindrance, like a treaty.
His entire contentment had become a routine,
Mountain rocks, naked green might be seen,
He gazed all the nook, in search of vision:
Finally he understand, he was blind,
And all the mercuric light was inside,
suddenly, he heard some unknown voice,
"I am hanging sound" was the answer, twice,
Appeared then drowsy-eyed clouds,
Beard, broad and proud,
Like red hot gold hoard,
Pumped like cotton transit bowl,
More like dark melted dross,
strictly stranded, still spouse,
To see, to seem, to seek a cause,
Clouds began the murmuring,
Echoing
And lightening,
Their static willing,
And dynamic whispering,
"Oh! he get the blink,
Of nature's praise,
Like solid gaze,
Transmogrified trace,
Which is compassionate,
Determined and definite,

Com'on let us lit,
A cheered lamp,
That may meet,
His destined path,
And deeply greet,
What can he bring?
Eminence and string,
visionary wing,
Absolute kink and ring,
Abysmal differentiated twin,
Human being,
Is that so easy?
NO, never that extreme,
Very oval and busy,
Like apparent dream,
With attiring frame,
Let me call it friend,
An en-written game,
Eloquence intend,
Bears capitalistic fame,
Riddling the read,
That naturally pear,
And scintillating souls breed,
Ceasing all fear,
Really hard to deem,
a self tormented shore,
And appraisal of dream,
No matter how hardcore,
Socialistic meteor,
Where are the hues?
Reality do not tire,

Some will give him clues,
With pondering and fire,
Pain will compel,
Which he feel,
Compassion reveal,
Having eternal pill,
Sorrow burns,
Tempest churns,
Secrecy turns,
Knowledge earns,
What can we say?
Alcoholic songs,
That he pray and tray,
Freezes into a bong,
Vanishes slowly,
Like fragrance,
Spread freely,
With winged fantasy,
Greasing brain,
Flushing breath,
Doing souls anatomy,
Let's hope and dream,
His enduring win,
Allow him to green,
Leafs and environs,
Tint in flowers,
Whispering all tone,
Before red that powers,
After violet of eternal zone."
Sailing Stall Soul with all weighing measures,
Converged into a bond of treasures,

Like a woodland blow a wind,

Over the spirited scale of fleshes and blood,

And the sand granules suddenly moved to stall,

As a quick mirror to install all apall,

Spirits started spotting and wandering,

To merge into a glow in the oceanic fever,

Hacked to pivot all the subdued systemic metal to favor,

Stall soul restored all the silent staring spirits,

To cloak their waves in the scales of silence,

Cheering a imperial joy and hues of transmogrified brains,

Customizing all his faithful cards cairns,

In the bottomless hour of sights,

In all the dark signaled corners ,

Powered with resonance and reluctance,

Of every waving spirit to come and go,

And again aroused to brighten all those material sands,

Stall Soul directed its spirits in shore,

To pass the tunnels of the pasts to appear anew,

Viscous spirits slipped into and ushered in a new day,

Of the new lively constraints of the world,

which they lively, followed and proceeded its will,

At all the stage of imperfect decree to resisting rill,

All the dazzling drops of the circulating spherical spirits to race,

Winging and waving to unplug the highest culmination of idleness,

In all the admiration, unblinking sums of the vibrant queries,

Stall Soul was eagerly pretending praises to all the duly spirits,

To bloom every fear from the hopeful rhythms

Break matter, of highly fragrant stems,

Accelerating with the speed of darkness,

And seemingly parted never ending ways of live veins,

To the wondrous and heavenly cycles, within the self.

Viscous clouds of the inherent spirits,

Unplugged from the indifferent Stall Soul heat,

Withe incense limpid but burning water,

And the folk flowers floating over fogs alter,

The fragrance of the tiding flower and water,

In the trespasses of the traveling Stall Soul,

Searching beyond the sparkles of the water drops,

Embarked with the brownish foams of luminaries,

Flashing scenery slated on the white leaves,

Twisted upon the adventurous tones of bees,

Like breathing out without nose bubbles of complex keys,

stringing their fictional scent sinked into the stall soul,

With all his profusion and salvation ,

Trekked the talk of the mysterious queendom of bees,

Also the stalking butterflies of the dim light fairies,

Weaving the dream of the scenic voyage of spiritual chorus,

Singing the song of the earthen spirit course,

The passage of the delicate enchantment of the meticulous word,

Evenly placed before the stall soul, a world of colourful odd,

Why rain punctured the climate finch,

The spinning charm of the spirit differ from pinch,

swinging winds distances greenish ups; down spring,

Growing shadows disappears with the focus of the Stall Soul string,

Surfing feathers waves down all the rhapsody crawl,

Before the mortal years travail the yearning world,

Dancing waves dissolves into the oceanic dew mourn,

Forlong a vanity was heckling the echoes of tempting flowers horn,

Beyond there was a distilling vista of gracious horizon,

A tempest monuments of the growing hills timbers,

Stall Soul entered the cavern chambers,

Profoundly asked the busy bubble bees and restricted butterflies,

About the the unsuited rhymes of the fortunes entropies,

A prized key fortune of rising and turning of the surrounding,

Which inserted the innocent and similar unwinding,

Whispered the bee and butterfly,

"When the endless dusk touches the sky,

The silence of the invisible laugh, correcting eye,

While the sacrifice of the sparks, however belittle knife ,

Can the convergence of nights and fights squeezes strifes?

Entrusts to keep the everlasting spiritual envy,

Will ensure the coloured dusk to collide with colour of eye,

Hey Stall Soul tough it is to assume the premature solutions."

Stall soul making the true sense around the moments,

Passed a soft voice for the secret key of the fortune,

"To deliver the equation of the intrinsic fairy"

Busy bees and restricted butterflies ,

Started spraying laugh towards the request of the stall soul,

Saying,"Dear, some chords of life is the image of the heart,

Unmindful of the aura and the sights of your spirits,

Not to outdo you a call before the waving stage,

Hey, you're a crazy phoenix,

Will turn the quest to higher winds,"

Denying the need of the equanimity of the answer,

Stall soul smiled and quietly thanked!

The busy bubble bees and restricted butterflies,

Whispered in the resonant voice,"phoenix",

Stall Soul moved forward in his intrinsic searching.A sauntering inn-ale of sequences were the next,

Stall Soul with all his clutched instinctive grounds,

Appears along the walking, purposeful life,

Conserved all the trump appetizers in a conceived motion?

Ree-vigorous was his published demonstration:-

Every individuals in the frivolous acting borders,

Designed to be assessed by the integral defender,

To approaching ill-fitted and surprized blinker,

An old cockroach in a mission to destabilize Stall Soul,

Got a thermal sock, when glanced a soul's stroll,

During the aimless grumble from the unresolved cockroaches,

The countless strings, reeling off the journey of coaches,

The antiquated pressures of wet jasmines lightened lances,

Admiring rusting tuples, Nor stills the thirsty graces,

Cockroaches forgot the dragging pillars of Stall Soul,

Indulges into trimmed tonics of Dexterity,

And their veil of vanity propelled in road's hasty,

Sects of yellow spirit vigor and endlessly pitched,

In clouds of stall-souls' cavalry, unseen of discord,

A cockroach distorted from the clouds asked,

To hypnotize Stall Soul deterred, dangled, masked,

Blazing the sum to lie down in the proof of dusts,

Started in-chanting in front of non-trust,

Vanquish thirst had growled the eyelid of stark Stall Soul,

Cockroach trembled and asked if illicitly to crawl,

Rhymes and beats sung to crawl, foments fall!

Behind the doors of novel heart__eerily husking stall soul-

Quite and fast asleep- pitching a single stroll,

Getting the hasten gesture-- the mad foment had passed.

Leaving a hustle of opaque drives horde,

Stall Soul seemed to past every faded face bod--

Clays of strings were dancing as evergreen grasshopper,

Ties of semantics were non-tired of tugging waves,

Even aromatic Stall Soul, seemed mislaid to pour away,

Stall Soul left drifters and all the faded face cue,

Devoid of woos and, yet knowingly said who?

Ordained a vital blue of the summarily dries,

The oceans in the Stall Soul readily arise,

Crashing waves itself displayed heavens--

Knighted lights, the rest of world could ever find?

The boundless degree of the en-act air,

Colossus hardly, in redeemed transience gear,

Shuffled card evermore, snap of the world,

To stall soul only a count of fugitive and troll,

Darting days into ceaseless storms of sky--

Couldn't help through the airy dry--elusive-en-light,

And one day from the livid shuffled cards,

four starters come down to play aside,

Softest Stall Soul candidly draw the cards beside,

Slowly arse the fortifying play to go a swarm,

Divinely spirited Stall Soul, separated the lesser cards,

Blistering stream of play deranged glances of pads,

Even dew shivered from the desert storms of the Phoenical-gray,

Not a seeker--playing pranks of pray,

Recovering snaps of reprieve from the digging hollow,

An old owl-ed card remains the cloudy--crow,

Fire shots of creek, dared the nights spree:

A blue fish card named peepul tree, in discorded entree,

Flashes ree-double, crashed a ballad of faking climax,

Every end space triumphed from the resonant of invincible Stall Soul Extol.

3. NOISY BIRDS

A cluster of noisy birds had their nests in my neighborhood,

Creating sound and complaining to one another, in a lyre fascinating mood,

Living in their nests, ex-halted and accumulated from dusts and disuse,

Feather and feather all around, growing like a feeble fuse,

In a bad conviction, not worthy was their dilapidated condition,

In a pathetic condition, their beautiful edifice was became a dirt creation,

With a coin of compassion in a merciful winter, finally ready for renounce reformation,

And they stringed some ventures of repair and transformation,

Yearning was passionate, full of foggy faith, but failed,

Because, in the mean time, their stupidity prevailed,

In the process of transformation, to get ephemeral joy and strive,

They tossed their nests, in a possession to thrive,

Despite their deep exertion of working in a profound,

One morning, they toppled their beautiful edifice in the ground, left me broken hearted,

For reasons, i have sympathy in my discerning heart with deep disgrace that halted,

Why did they pulled the whole edifice in the ground?

Why did they not cleared restored and get their home self-absorbed?

Why did they not seek for permanence, and establishment?

What was reform, really meant to them?

Was that the desolating, separating from the old soiled frame?

It is still haunting and surprising me silently with fussiness,

Does reformation transit to renovation to partial perfection or demolishing to freshness?

4. A TIME MACHINE

More than a decade ago, i bought a watch,

From the nearby crept and steady marketplace,

Watch was beautiful, with stripes in match,

Blue short hand and red long hands, in grace,

That gave me immense pleasure and delight,

It suited me nicely with all its fancy feature,

A few days passed, of its strange insight,

Things started reacting, and with changing creature,

More days passed now exist a new sprigged world,

On a moist earth of gloomy shade,

Turfed a new surface, thronged a different crowd,

A worried species full of space and clouded haze,

Of all melancholy, that hold them bright,

Meteoric power blossoms to their standstill hope,

Like some deity technocrats, steadfast with glory,

Some like to glorified and called them democratic,

Few were sober priests of socialism,

Few were divinity of crowned capitalism,

And most of them matted to mixed thought,

Loaded with industrial access,

All of them eventide of it and with similar thoughts,

Contracted the outer bubble with polluting poison drought,

Grounded the earth itself, to a diluted different earth,

Polluting the ground water, barren-ed the earth in dearth,

Now every oblivion was secret spy against nature's horizon,

That needled my soul, and battled my emotion,

I glanced at well wooing sun, it was thirsty,

With terrorized and over brimmed man's amnesty,

All were unjustified and had eternal dew,

Mountain to mass all set to unmew,

They tried to spread their frecked wing,

But failed due to fogged dusty wind,

Which enveloped me in a burden with thoughts of firmament,

That kept me helpless, raising all the temperature's tenement,

Nothing was there to whizz the lonesome loneliness of a yacht,

Uplifting a brighter vision, spangled my weird watch,

Which had exalted me to a ceased world, between time and space-

Oh! That quivered me to hate my watch, of discoursed continuity,

As it forced towards the terrorized environs and its fearful melody,

Now, all its tint were bad, my slow time machine was bad!

Now, all its silvery settings were rusted, and gone in eld,

Missing all its splendour, suddenly i waked up,

I was lying on my bed beside course books, stalled and wrecked up,

Contesting with each other, like beauty crest,

Now that i understand, it was only a dream departed,

A driving dream of life, light and time which halted,

And left me some unstable, opaque questions of eager spirits;

Could i get that watch in real or was that paused and painted imagination?

Is any watch can be a 'slow time machine' or was that a dream of comic hallucination?

For sure, it was a nascent self tormenting dream of joy departed.

5. DEEP INSIDE THE OCEAN

• 29 •

Deep inside the ocean, visibility has a new definition,

Some strange city of atrocities and third kind of vision,

Deep inside the ocean evolve a lurid sea region,

Resembled and redesigned stripes of darkness creation,

Blended with turret shadows of heaven and hell, gaping season.

6. TURNING STOIC

Bending sky to a distant land,
Tugging like life's crystal,
Discrete life's lustrous shine,
Tagging like shrine petal,
Silent songs dissolve in even-
Expanding air, a myriad bloom,
Outface a passionate impression,
To the gears of roses, feasibly fume,
Add little drops of honey,
To the saline Aquarius world,
Let acquire softness to feel,
Distill the whole hurled,
Only a precipitous zeal,
Lingers the day, O dear,
Emotional fountains are vocal,
Engrave a hoping fear,
Like fish swing on the surface,
Gulling temperance trace,
Firmly Subtend and bend,
Now, be disunion of fence,
Never paused enduring forms,
In the corals amidst life stride,
Infinite cloak of retaining crest,
Abyss dialogue conjugates aside,
When filling equanimity,
Of daring senses to humble scene,
Noble thrills of a image defy,

All worldly cracks and fancy pie,
Variable silence of human head,
Aiding little free spire,
Invisible can convulse,
Only when one way turns dire,
To induce myopic logs level,
Life is gala day of logistics,
Sometimes silently magnify dark,
Diving pain and fear stoics,
Listening dismay in way,
Inscribe an aromatic hollow,
Heart's yearning, surfing waves,
Like a lighthouse radar, does hello.
Every blitz of rare tints,
Ooze curly rays of blinks,
Blazed with fancied desires,
Eternal smoke like a soul twinks.

7. DANCING HILLS

Sloppy air of the nearby dancing hills,
Up, down and murky as modesty drills,
As the hurry winds, friskily caress to pass,
Sounding cheers, drizzled inside a message to grasp,

Remembrance of dusty road, and old ways,
Constantly ripples, vow to show, delighted old days,
With few paddles and cycling along rectified curves,
Blissfully breath cool smileys in each nerves,

The murmuring sound of the hillside waterfall chain,
Sprinkle a wave to sooth tirelessly traveling vein,
Summarily myths of low-lying lazy clouds, burst a bit,
Circute an endless journey, from the passage orbit.

8. NATURAL INSTINCTION

n-variance follow perfect incrustation,
Throughout length and breadth of generation,
When seeking gaze give a willing due,
Likeliness not easily reflect a twilight as true,
Lounging life at the tip of strangers,
Hardly facsimile just by tossing the fingers,
History of illustrations envelope mind with light's speed,
Invoke for seekers, trekking for life's bid,
Natural instinction project a clustered heart bind,
Ambling directives to profound for the order of mind,
Even alteration, code and credits mind to react,
Selects the musing pictures on mirroring heart act,

9. THE FAITH OF THE FLOWER

When the fascinating flowers of the fall,
Swiftly toppled to rill and roll on the grounds floor,
Faint with the traversal of the old frequent winds atoll,
Ramps and reminds all the lyrical memoir,
To sage the morning mild dew fuse and free,
Laying vigorously on the damp soil and green grass,
Perfumed and springing to sort a season glee,
Offering a grace of rewind at the spraying shine,
The perch of the ballooning branches of the tree,
Unaware of the hurtfulness of the flowers' faith,
Sailing unknowingly elsewhere in the onus sky's entree,
Tossing logistics to chisel the happening prose,
Of the experiment in every perch of the saline treasury,
And softly spiked a wind to kill its dim dream to browse,
Filled with all high spirited hoping degree,
An echo of silence trans-versed in thoughts,
By the awakening, traversal of the entire day,
Destined till the evening experience of the pain,
And the curtain fall, outdo a certain call-
The bird's heart could not understand the budding flower's brain.

10. EARTHLY PRISON

Why not fly in the infinite sky?
Why?Look at the dense, veined wings!;
Pretending powers of imagination,
Obtusely outgrows from the heart,
Why not forget this earthly prison;
Full of fogged followers Of gravity,
Mesmerizing me to the whole world;
Of glassy airy colors,
Which magnetize relevance by right,
And one bright morning,
Fueled with inner light and sight,
Would walk in the infinite sky.

11. AUTUMN LEAVES

Quarreling with the misty airy autumn,
The autumn leaves leave,
Often orient and gradually discorded,
Fall with the vanquish charm and believe,

Compromising with the misty airy autumn,
The autumn leaves leave,
Curling in the sunshine and shadowy night,
Self-propel and escape the tree with the dew,

Cosmification with the misty airy autumn,
The autumn leaves leave,
During crispy crude colours of the milky dawn,
Stirling and mixing with the visuals of the eve,

Sublime with the misty airy autumn,
The autumn leaves leave,
Jointing a graceful degree of scenes,
Unheard visions of the critical heart heave,

Voiding with the misty airy autumn,
The autumn leaves leave,
Creating hopes for the butterflies and birds,
Vacating fragrance as a natural grieve.

12. SWITCHED ON THE WALL

Have you seen natural reflections?
It can be conditionally colorful,
For sure, it needs an interface or reflecting surface,
A retreat to observe,
But when it is black, dark, crude,
Is it switched on the wall as a critic?

13. A LIGHTENING FIREFLY

A firefly in a jingling, singing mood stood,
Lingering a melodious song of tribal wood,
Mobilizing mutely and withholding silent siren, itself,
Stripped on every blink, unhidden, on table, on shelf,
Toppling in the sample space of inclusion and belief,
Let things ionized with stupendous glow, elif,
Came near a uppish headed, auguring ant,
Imbibing like a tiny rock-roll, and faint,
Sweeping slowly, shortly in course of meal-act,
Relatively a common constant, unreasoning fact,
Absolutely like radically magnetizing itself,
If it reached grocery and strive chill help,
The firefly stopped to ask the ant,
Aye! dear you work hard and instant,
A timeless template for the affinities,
of sweet and sugarcane, not suffered from diabetes?
The modern ant candidly replied the friend fly,
Do not you know, plausible fusible guy,
"It's so, that's why, very shortly, we die",
Said the ant, and thanked it for doctoring advice,
The fearless firefly moved to another pragma dice,
A resilient spider, weaving web cascade,
Tangling and cycling its leg on airy bed,
Exponentially expanding a macro bit overhead,
Queried the firefly mad, in more gestural interest,
why spider had famished and flimsy fate,
The arrogant spider vouched quickly in second,

Ye! conspicuous friend,"I don't have lightening wand",
And dared the frightened firefly to cross the quadruple,
Dared not the firefly, nifting its life double,
Convening its life and magic potion to all ardent friend,
Restlessly moved to all atypical trend,
Finding hints of all anomalies, few tall, few bend.

14. A FOGGY DAY

A foggy day often blind eyes!
Syrupy cold wind in a foggy day,
Flinching all muted sight,
Accordingly freeze, varying the vision,
Weather to see inner intuition of might,
Wispy winds implodes reasoning,
Aroused and abrupt, aware of a way away,
Consciousness in the unconscious crash,
Envoy of the dizzy brain in a decoy,
To conclude and let pass,
Before the resonating light rewind,
Do mirroring of self, all around,
With only gateway to en-cash the mind,
Once one could see only one onto many,
And dodged to see like him,
Ah! but those differed in crude fog,
Repose hidden fractions, ignored to vanish,
All are fractiously fogged,
Used to! tranquilize other,
All are consciously cloaked,
Used to! synchronize self.

15. SPIRITUAL FREEDOM

• 41 •

Let the freedom be freed,

From the assuming proportions,

Let the lights of true believe assimilates,

Through chiseling and modeling of notions,

Let the extensive flow glows under high brilliance,

And the freedom of spirit be exalted in country celebrations.

16. THE JUNGLE HISTORY

Once upon a time in the jungle history,

And a good green, testimonial time it was,

Naturally growing trees of wild beasts' story,

Centred in the circular array of living prose,

Nature face was foamed in the fanatical form,

In cold and mild aspirations of ecosystem,

Animals;Progressing purely on each other norm,

Running ripples, to burst for the existed esteem,

Man came, heavily exploited the nature and norm,

Joys impart, started sick season of global warming,

Led to the disastrous flood in the jungle to mourn,

The melodious hymns turned to crumbled cries,

But non linguistic creatures found- no heartfelt emotions,

And drowned with their bleeding heart to finally fail,

The razor-sharp reasons of man could not help devotions,

In between, Two jungle friends, shared a tale-

A fox with daring hope climbed up the tree,

A drowning deer was endeared and feared in the rocks,

The mild friend fox, poisoned parroted philosophies of life's mystery,

Could not save its life, the fanaticism of helpless fox?

17. SONG OF BAND OF TOADS

Rinsing, Roaming of the riddle rain,

Run from the cool clouds den,

To hit the earth in dragging trend,

Drumming of sticky rain,

Again and again,

One stares to chill,

Cooling the nerves with rainy cane,

One coagulate to peel the trouble,

Believing in the ban of rain to finally gain,

One vigor lividly for Love's sakes,

To heartily rhythm all songs of sane,

One triggered of the emotional brink,

Waiting for rain to quietly sooth pain,

Rain, come and go in a mystic way,

To let us know its mask of fashion remain.

18. STAYING WHITE

• 44 •

Hands-on start of plain peace process,
Leave the self gathered outbreak,
And assemble in calm quest,
Make it circular in lean jest track,

Peace never excel without rest,
Then convey, life and light,
Help the friend and the foe to approach,
without any reproach and taunt, staying white.

19. LIGHT SPIRITUALITY

• 45 •

Look at the dawn,

Immensely encored and clouded,

Accumulating dynamo to produce darkness,

To pass, how corp and crop,

With never ceasing permeation of thought,

And peace of mind, no fire, no sword,

Producing effect as morning dew,

Unseen and unheard,

Yet fascinate world of thoughts,

As spirituality of light,

Remove clotted darkness in a sight.

20. JUSTICE HAS NOT YET BEEN DONE

These earthly border drips the mind's sorrow,
Next, north west to my nation carry brutal arrow,
Hopes of peace are thirsty in dry dunes azureus,
And intensely, they ignore its innermost darkness,
Ego razors hardly cares of even oddly own-self,
Despite there encored, ever-growing, being true self,
Whose paused cares, scratched the face of humanity,
In many mortal time, deluding their own pride in haste,
Supporting evil is desperate distress, dispassionate,
One worriedly thinks if these fire could deride and burn,
As they shun terror, and justice has not yet been done.

21. REFORM MUST BE...

• 47 •

Casts must be,
Castism need not.
Sects must be,
Sectarianism need not.
Extreme must be,
Terrorism need not.
Truth must be,
Unjustified truth need not.
Faith must be,
Superstition need not.
Belief must be,
Hypocrisy need not.
God must be,
Being God need not.
Activity must be,
Outdated principles need not.
Uprising must be,
Immoderate revolt need not.
Ratiocination must be,
Broadening gaps need not.
Idea must be,
Idealism need not.

22. MODERATE MISCELLANEOUS

A caravan of vacuum glimpses,
Retorting in the counters of mind,
To tether the daring dreams,
Unto destiny, crowding senses to rewind,

A spring whistle entangled for coverage,
Why not without shadows of sound?
Mistakes are mysteries convene,
To draw equally in social bound,

Not ever objects in the universal ocean?
Like few moderate miscellaneous, where,
Creatures are readily rebel,
Nevertheless, the yearning is fair.

23. ALL ALONE

Poor uttering virtuous mirror,
Visualize a image,
Showing all perspective to admire,
Self centered persona to circulating mirage.
All the center provoking each grown,
Negotiating, preponderating with courage,
Waiting to pursue mind's digraph,
Why trembled randomly,
A distance is turning in full half ,
Between day and night afar,
Holding it untold and ceased,
En-wrapped in a trivial point star,
Like some nestling lies, but true,
Shadowing all alone,
Waiting standalone and calmly.

24. IMAGINARY WINGS

Hope is a visionary experience:
All of it, all dis-rented indifference,
A pretense whispering of discontent,
Multitudes of time and space inheritance,

Hope is a tempering wizard:
Tempered like a switch of dismal trough,
Electrifying the soul to brighten first most,
And tranquilizing the inner self,

Hope is noble nature's inception:
possessing a instinctive joy of influence,
Welcoming heart, to make believe,
And rekindle the general gradiance,

Hope is a solemn soul's soother:
Controlling choice in flowing pain,
And helps the agitating heart to drink,
Because nature has confined it with fancy fun,

Hope is imaginary wings of faith:
Fly fast in search of solace spring,
Like bees melody for their nectar hive,

Neither kneeling nor noting, nor sing.

25. ARCH FOR EVOLUTION

Eminence crudely overcast a hindrance,
Can it thicken a voluminous grace?
What makes an appetite silent insensate?
Why is hope the only companion to compensate?
How are doldrums diabolically dwells in between?
Queries in arch for evolution are perplexedly keen:
To knowledge, kindled by candle within fence,
To Learning, as average aviator has no frame,
To mistakes, merely a favourite complain,
When not scarcely seemed, otherwise a vain,
A philosopher peace could not be depicted,
Until, redundancy radically in-tempted,
Yet, dream apprises to forward faith like envoy,
Whatever would come, joy or envy.

26. A TIGER'S TALE

A very fairy tale of a tiger terror's tail,
At young boyhood age he had long hopeful nail,
In eternal hues, unknown of strife,
Living happily in vivid colors of life,
Awakened his spirit on other wilds,
Remain still and composed, he was really mild,
Getting gladness, upon the entropy of echoing earth,
Strong, calm, monotonous,since his birth,
He had a philosophy, 'chaous will definitely bring the morrow',
And deep passion fitted him, with nomadic sorrow,
From fierce foes, fleeting into peace to hustle,
He decided to wander the nearby jungle,
But, some old skin tigers were already there,
Giving him a local gesture, looked out when saw the peer,
In their happiest day of happiest hour,
He asked them of their residential pride and power,
As the first glance assured, definitely had ever seen,
The old knew him, offered the red meat they had been,
He stood and asked in an astonishing chilled voice,
Where they had come, if they knew him ancestor-wise,
They greeted mutely, in old reserved speech,
Surfacing all glance, brightening all breeze,
And replied so silently, in a cross questioning grace,
If he knew lifeless stands, that they were actually ghosts,
He had not interpreted them convincingly,in truest,
That seemed very jocular, he laughed while breathing air,
Taking it false and low, transcendent in consciousness pair,

Throwing back to the old, that was not possible in real,
In very circumstances he was not acquainted with that rill,
The old were self sprinkled, bounced it back,
Depicted his woodland bounds, coursing his gaiety trait,
Dialed all moral round, Interpreted indifference, and quoted,
In a carol wild,"then, you are a ghost".

27. CONVEYOR

Is winning always a surplus action?
Let it by consciousness and compassion.

Is desire a rummaging fiction?
When one know not the paternal, leaser attraction.

Is apathy a distillation of fear?
Then, multitudinous can be a compass conveyor.

28. THE EARLY SCENE

When there were no birth on earth, random hushed,
No human being not a single one fused,
Land was bewildered by augmented animals,
Crawling, creeping, creatures of vanity, produced.

There were trees, in full fonts, no worthy worries,
They had hands and gum-shields, so lividly,
Their content comradeship,
A tree township triumphed truly.

Sky had disciplined flying screaming swifts,
Moving and marshaling in algorithm,
Categorized in column one, two and eight,
In chattering, colored, vibrant, viscous air in rhythm.

Limpid blue water had another wisdom,
Slippery shadows to creature shine,
Like a predominant acting world, with foments,
With swimming ghosts as preponderating villain.

When nature adored the change convene,
Amusing animals retrieved all its feature,
Adopted all its creation for being human,
Started burgeoning, hustle to horde, like animator.

Trees kingdom departed, assured human,
Fissured its hand, shuted its mouth-shield,

Others, unamused were restricted in jungles,
Forced oceans to draw its water,escape more land.

Hence, man redeemed, partitioned the early scene,
Disintegrated the earth, accordingly used and excused,
Land, water and air, indebted from nature, unpaid,
Noble nature, negotiating and mending with the mused.

29. TO MAINTAIN AND RESTRAIN

Peace in fear can lean,

Rusted nested nations, with pin,

Nature not green,

Improvisers are not keen,

Society in egging ego, mean,

Faith in scream,

If aroused within,

Could be of greatest help and use!

Let the world arouse to gain,

Peace again,

Nature like heaven,

Society, must be humane,

In selfless manner, all in beautiful pane.

To maintain and restrain,

Let the world to gain,

The greatest oneness!

30. POLITICAL PERFECTIONN

Moderation these days has frill forecast,
To improve imperfection among vast,
Politically, perfection is circular cast,
Through pernicious dots and two way past,
Diffused and desolated, jocularly at last,
Yet perfect, compassionate in big contrast.

31. COSMIC CHORUS

In a cosmic event organized by God,
Many universe alighted to spread aromatic tone,
A beleaguered galaxy as a late night host,
Started singing, swooping to win the heart most;
Visualized, human's cosmic change, charm podcast,
Of amiably earthly echoes of tryst.

God showered in moonlights, nectar sweet,
Answered at last in a singing fairies;
Sometimes looping darkness explore a glaze,
Like variation in the blinking pulsating phase,
The 'blue planet' called earth is a case;
A flying feat with emerald mist marketplace,
Illuminated by cosmic chorus and its own silver shades!

32. AN ENSHRINE TALE

• 61 •

To Google a myth in a dusty dodged road,

Determined to find a destination,

Anguish in gesture with hefty hope,

Simmered and stopped by a staggering station.

Moved again in a perennial searching,

Trekked the renewed rainbow,disgraced but meek;

whizzed the sky through draining rain,

Mortal years passed in jaded job to seek,

Unturned myriad mysteries and timeless ages,

Dared beyond the blues, slippery shadows in marine,

To know the system of solitary spirits,

But, oh life! Unanswered, wearied and enshrine

33. OFF BUDS

Hoped Grasshopper carrying daylight,
Make decimal gaps,
A much needed toad, in snake's mouth,
Laugh wittingly to collapse;

Into a punctured shell,
A snail speedily enters to mend,
An unaware famished bird,
Smile to hunt and bend;

Not the secrets of jasmine,
Amorous ants doors,
Scratching with cursive pencils,
Sees bees of duly chores;

A butterfly wants to buy sky,
Must past the thwarted needle,
Timely flowers at ten O'clock
Carved from unknown tunnel.

34. DIM YET APPEAR

Who traces last delusions of the evening stark,
When sunshine ends wasting into dark,
By deftly shunning the dropping noise afar,
Solid crystals of everyday pondering star,

Who traces the waves of world on race;
Roars of the salty water on funny face,
Fare ships frozen in the amid cold air,
Rainbows in the curves of the waterfall were,

Who traces these wanderer bird;
Professing to pick and rill straws, ironed hard,
Springing desires outlasts in heartily displays,
Sorts of the blue and clear sky, endeared here,

Who traces all the cemented life sway;
Bars prisoning the globe with temp ray,
Resistive rests of the dew and fogging fuse,
Amid dreams resounding in the wings of rose,

Who traces from the unknown nodes head-on;
Lightening thunders to prized and poised run,
Awaiting arrows of the lovelorn hearts,
Tight ropes of hopes, mightier than just parts,

"I'm" genetics of ego don't revolve these to self.

35. A VILLAGER

A villager focus to ardent incident,
Just to know the fastening raining paint,
Without cordial balancing swift arm,
Pace of wind softening in warm,

He knew all tricks reasonable,
From the trees and leaves amiable,
Aiding tradition to open green space,
Never adapted of dwelling bad spring air-ace,

Is the eternal voice of nature shatter,
when the triumph responses in appreciator,
The syrupy large cloud undimmed,
Even the radial violating string amped,

One day, villager would drawn in readily dusk,
while-in grounded, an ending ignition of the sun,
Norton star, By the day, Hold a burning grin,
Tingled blood, prized rest to the day's engine.

36. SOMEONE HAD DROPPED INK FROM THE CANDLE

Waving Knights entered in the sly,
Stars strictly civilized in the sky,
Stick upon mountain face,
Urbanized ultimately in brilliance,

The stars shining through the dark cellulite,
Field the earthly corners with eerie light,
Twisting freely in the harmonic tune,
Suspect alone in gazing immune,

Thrilled appreciation may happen afar,
Between chuckled chained star,
Despondence slowly, unrelated rhythm drive,
Ebbed slowly, seemed hot, tired and bellowed drive,

Some sleepy stars dis-trace away,
Let their habits, risking the day,
Stars transfixed in music sensing and eating,
Leapt chances, as took away a motorbiking,

Tempt of musical hope in disgraced heart,
Toured in all the dotted colored part,
Someone infinitely, lightened universal puddle,
Someone had dropped ink from the candle!

37. FORBIDDEN UNIVERSE

For the immaculate treasure,

Hidden from the universal ages,

Reviewed and resounded force erasers,

Minus eccentric fugal and petal cages;

Transform into yellow flowers,

Of reflective source and willing sink of universe,

Bemused before the lamp shades,

Deeper then the dark sink heads,

Behind the moderated edges,

Mortals, biding introspection glimpses,

Listening to white noise of morning bird,

Can yet kindled the weird night mud,

Now, the slope of cubical era,

Paving the peerless path of manifested universe,

Playing the mystic vision of global pole,

Floating around, drawn every soul,

Glory within, jingling of sandy shores softly done ,

Leisure denying dreams to trespass dawn.

38. WAXED

Arrival of subtle colors invoked,
On half hearted waves of lives,
Floating on the plotted battles,
With the rating mint of airy dives,

Figures of philosophy is unknown,
When passing days cubically peddles,
Thin dreams often transits truth,
Sings fragment of broken vessels,

Far beyond the sky and earth,
Highlighted against waxed scheme,
Why crab crawls in a market box,
To grab each other,showing peer steam.

39. A COLOURED FLASH

A leading destination in a awaited way,
Headed in a dappled, voluminous light day,

All the stuffs bloomed in camps of rivers,
Through the arches of lances, influencing divers,

There are whistling fogs, unconquered in the seasons flow,
Cunning to slide the view of the willing air to do...

Feathers startled to draw an airy arched sun,
To whirl a true shadow of the way unknown.

40. MIND'S NATURAL WIRE

· 69 ·

Share and like buttons to enhance a primitive view,
At all the crossroads, does symbols matter anew?
Not to foster a way to privilege, agitate a less dense take,
Awe-struck, other unequal reviews, inherited posterity as fake,
Life is short, matters most, must for wants and desire,
Lively allocate as assimilate and grow with mind's natural wire.

41. SLIPPERY GROUNDS

A metal bestowed in the zeal sun,
Galloped all the twist to radiate,
And parted on rested raid, taking run on,
Every setting shades into the whirlpool, deviate,
When awaited for a damp music of ghosts to plot,
In the continuity of slippery grounds,
Like a vehement stirring in the loaded life's pot,
Into the aloofness, and tagged cage bounds,
In the vorticity of colors, precipitately as it rose,
And magnetized to spin within,
Outcast a calm circumstance to chose,
Ever solace, steadfastly, Invincibly, run to curtain.

42. HOOTING IN THE HEART OF HEART

When the encircled ends of rolling dote,
Stack onto amount an accelerated turn,
Filled motions of charming wondrous routes,
Relieves all the running path a ticket to earn,

By the way, a hanging town allied,
staggered by lonely cottages, equally bright,
In day and night of the fluctuating time,
An antique theme of lives, restored at the height,

Not so far the vibrant music of the dusk,
Looping surrounding sounds of bells around the neck,
Of the grazing and gazing cows and goats,
Stalking a glazed music in life's deck,

A little eye smoke are undermined from its dynamics,
Pumping a peculiar sound of compassionate throw,
From faces to walking gulls to clanging iron gates,
All smoked with hidden bright and dark shadow,

When mooted and mocked eyeing of sinuous shadows,
Lividly enlarge and grilled onto one and once,

With slow twists and tangled search of a magnifier,
Seems to be torched as unbreakable silent customer,

Spraying white paints of fathoming nature,
Opened all the quite worldly window pane,
The unknown servitude become cores enthralled,
Scrolling the deep springs of emotional brain,

To every questing core of the hearts,
Hooting in the heart of heart, expanding remote grime,
Even the deepest chords of the distilling heart,
Is Flying in the innocent blue sky and propitious time.

43. FINITE WAKE

A thick, soft and swift ethereal air,
Stir viscous on friendly finite wake,
Opened a vision for the heavenly hanging environs,
Fictitiously and virtuously swing for sweet sake,
The ethereal air pretend and trend,
On the tricky ticking sand of shiny environs
Days passes ethereal air lost sights,
In crossing seasons of tabular slate,
Wandering about each take aright,
Environs takes empty wonders ways,
And decide a run with ethereal air,
Turns into course to complete,
So environs are not good in long race gear.

44. LIVE DREAMS

• 74 •

Invigorated veins visits effervescent vessels,

Whenever to wake the winsome tales,

Like a concrete licker lizard , silently whistles,

Incorporating the modular meal to swallow bites,

May be a decisive mirror to pass into,

Or shell to the another worldly ocean,

Just by slipping legs on crests too,

Brighter than the slippery sand granules of invariable times,

Even-ting the probables to monumental desire,

To transverse beyond inner beyond affinity,

Of infinite shiny spirited colorful sky-smoke fire,

Ejected by a flying yacht of drunkard's moon city,

Like a flutter of all comprehension in details,

Distinctive nature to dive in caves of dark corners,

Curling amiably to all misfortune desire bells,

Amplified live dreams of highly concentrated spirits,

Crystal poured, to cross the attracting saturation pairs.

45. PAINTED WORKPLACE

• 75 •

Lifted down the weightlessness of a thought,
That already had a outward way of cordial craft,
Many times things make matter like the false jest as true,
When bonded hope bit are the best form of clue,

When it sunk deeper and deeper,
To find the destination of truth not that bitter,
For the unknown and uncovered faces in mystery,
How to melt the mind cotters, ado all to free,

In the lattice of minds indefinite crystal,
Flowing thoughts have ranges to cover metal,
Anyways memories are the painted workplace,
With goodness of good, bad turns of days in grace.